What It Is Like As A Transgender Boy In The 1960's and 1970s

By
Terry Virgil

Table of Content

Chapter One

Introduction

In the 1960's if was forbidden for a boy to even wear girl's clothing, but in my case it was real weird having others just think I was a girl, when in truth I never even tried to look or even dress like a girl, but yet other thought I was a girl for some reason why.

Okay maybe it had to be the fact I was dressed by my mother as a watch for Halloween when I was in the first grade, or it has to deal with my first name; who knows and I will never know, and nor shall you ever know why.

Here is just one fact that is even weird for me that even playing in a playground where I grow up the girls would come to me and say I should have bigger thighs as a girl. Okay I was a very shy boy at the time and this is a little weird to be classified as a girl when I was only six years old.

Here is one other fact that there was a lady that live not too far from my house and she did one thing that would get others to think I was a girl. She invited me to her house and gave me some girls clothing to try on and I could have if I would like them. She even liked having over to her house wearing girl's clothing, and she even told me I am a very pretty little girl, and as a girl I should be wearing girls' clothing more because I looked very sweet.

Okay I told you about how my mother did make a watches costume for Halloween, but I did not tell you that I was wearing girl's undergarments like panties, and a t-shirt that was made for a girl to wear. Oh yes I even wore girl's shoes and tights with a nice black wig.

Now because of the watch's Halloween costume and wearing that to our Halloween party at school the girls all accepted me as a girl, so did the boys, and my teacher, and here is why.

Okay I had to ride the bus to school and even the older kids on the bus treated me as a girl. I can even recall that one of the older girls' saying that it was about time I would wear a dress because I was a girl. It was one of the bigger girls' that said I was very pretty and I should wear more dresses and she even thought that I was a girl from the beginning; she even added that I should not be as shy as a girl. She was one of my neighbors that got on at the very same bus stop as I did.

There was one thing that did happen before the Halloween party at school with my Teacher she would not even allow me to use the boy's bathroom, or she caught me trying to use the boy's bathroom and I was told I must use the girl's bathroom because girl's are not allowed to use the boy's bathroom or Locker room. I never understood this before when I was a child, and yes I did not know how to read in the first grade when I started the first grade. There was no such thing as a girl's symbol on either the boy's or girl's bath room in the 1960's to make things a lot easier for a boy to know just where to go. I could also say having a pink name tag to mark where I was to sit in my classroom was also confusing. I was even told I had to play with the rest of the girls because as a girl all girls should play with girls only. This was a norm for kids in the 1960's

My grandmother did a few things that would be considered very interesting for me. She made me shirts to wear with rounded collars and ruffles on the collars, and pink in color. She knew I was a boy, and boys' do not wear a rounded collar that is ruffled and pink, for pink is for girls and blue is for boys. My grandmother did this by the way as well. She likes to bake and wanted to teach me how to bake, and cook. Well here is the strange part about me learning how to bake and cook. My grandmother had me wear girl's clothing. Yes she had some old cloths that did not fit my aunt anymore and had me try them on and wear them to bake and cook. The

4

reason was that she did not want to see my cloths get dirty and seeing that boys are not to learn how to bake and cook in the 1960's that meant I had to wear a dress or skirt in order to do work that a woman or girl did around the house. I even had to dress as a girl when it came time to help my grandmother do the laundry. The laundry got hung outside on the cloth line, and that is the very first time my grandmother's one neighbor's daughter saw me and asked if I could play with her. My grandmother said yes, but I had to change my cloths. I can recall this from that girl. She said it was okay for we were just going to play house and she did not know I was a boy. To her I was another girl to play with. So I went to her house and began to play house.

The girl had a brother as well and he said this to me I think. I wanted to know why I had short hair. I don't know what I said to him but I can recall his sister asking if he would join us to be the daddy.

Her parents did invite me to dinner for they liked the fact I was a new friend to both their daughter and son. I accepted their invitation, but first I had to tell my grandmother and see if it was okay. She did say yes as long as I would change just before my grandfather saw me dressed as a girl. Now I had to change in the clump of tree that separated my grandparent's property and their neighbor's property.

It was from that time I first wore dresses or skirts in front of my grandmother I would wear them a lot in front of her and my grandparents neighbor's too, but note this they never even found out that I was a boy all this time, for every time I would visit my grandparent's I could dress as girl and play with them until I was a teenager. Of course my grandparent did die when I was a teenager, and yes I did miss dressing up as a girl too.

Okay I would wear a dress or skirt when I would visit my grandparent's and learn how to be a girl, who ever my grandfather die first then my grandmother, and yet she did see me dressed as girl in two play that I was in the first one when I was in fourth grade in the musical play "HMS Pinafore", and I was fourteen when I played Laurey Williams in the musical play "Oklahoma" both I will tell you about at a later time in the book, and why I had to play both parts and just how that went. Now we are going to stay with my early or the beginning on my life as a boy dressed and me passing as a girl.

Okay I did mix up the beginning here in the introduction part of my book, but as you can see I am going by my memory, but it should give you the reader just how something like this would happen to a person like me. You should also keep in mind I kept all of this as a secret for everyone even my very own parents and the rest of the family or any of my friends.

Being a very shy boy did help me keep these things as a secret, for I did not like to talk about anything at all, for being shy is just the type of boy I wanted to be from my early years of life. Here is one fact I never told what was on my mind at all, or how I felt. I never even told any when I felt sick.

Now I just gave you some idea of just how I was as a boy that could pass as a girl, and just how I got started wearing girl's clothing and just how weird it was for me because I was passing as a girl or having other think I was a girl without them even knowing that I was a boy.

I have to say passing as a girl like I did without trying I wish I knew just what others where seeing when they saw me. I wish I knew if they saw my body as one of a female of was I just the right shape to pass as a girl.

Okay I did say I would tell you just how I the part in a musical play called "HMS Pinafore" and played the part "Little Buttercup".

The reason and how I became "Little Buttercup" from the musical play "HMS Pinafore" is one thing that seems out of the ordinary, for some reason the musical teacher had me singing as a soprano, well the only boy in the soprano section in music class in the fourth grade. She always through that I was a girl. Yes I had long hair like a girl would back in the 1960's blond in color.

In truth being a very shy boy did also help me land the role as "Little Buttercup" in the musical play "HMS Pinafore", for I did not even want to be in the play at all, but I was told everyone will be in the play, and there was not one thing I could do about that. There was just one simple problem and it was my parents. Now my parents could not read at all and with that in mind they wanted to say something about play a female role in a musical play, but they just did not say anything and let me play the role "Little Buttercup". So I now began to even pass as a girl in public and on a stage too.

Instead of having everyone's parent make their own costumes, the school had a professional makeup artist and professional costume person make our costumes for the musical play.

The good thing for me is that I did not have to wear and girl's undergarments under the dress that I was wearing, but I had to wear shoe of the time period, so my shoes where costume made, plus I had to wear tights. My mother kept my dress tights, and shoe that I had to wear on stage. Well mom like to keep all these things as keep sake and to prove that I was in the musical play in the fourth grade. She even kept the still pictures of me on stage.

The next time I would be on stage was when I was fourteen in 1968 as "Laurey Williams" in the musical play "Oklahoma" and yes I was even shy back then.

In the fifth grade I was asked out on a date by a boy that thought I was a girl. We had a thing call safety patrol whereby a safety patrols person help kids cross the streets safely. Okay I did not go on the date, but I asked him why he asked me out on a date. His answer was is that he thought that I was a girl, and a very cute girl. He even said something like this that other boys even thought that I was a very cute girl too.

Now that you have an idea about my back ground just what is was like being a boy in the 1960's when others were thinking that I was a girl or other has that idea.

In the next chapter you will read the more deal and things that did happen to me to me later on in life and in school when other was thinking I was a girl and even more like one thing that happen to me was the reaction that came after September 7th 1968.

Chapter Two

The School play

In chapter two we are going to talk just a little bit more about what it was like for me as a boy whereby something may seem out of order but keep in mind that I am writing this from my memory, and yes my memory is very shape. So I can remember things very well. In this chapter I will tell you things from my teen years.

Let us start when I was fourteen years old in 1968 and go to the point when I was in school when the liberals and feminist movement was growing real big across the United States of America.

This was the year of a new type of education system about to start. It was the year of what is called co-ed education, women's right marches, and other liberal movement ideas.

The liberal ideas is one thing that I never liked and never will like, for it was the liberal movement that turned me into a very conservative man; for I did recognize the fact that all liberal things are wrong and will always be wrong. Even with the idea of co-ed education, or laws like the California bathroom law.

The effect of the liberal movement is what turned me from being a very shy boy to the man that I am today, not shy at all. Here is one thing I have no fear of anyone or anything that happens to be in the world.

Okay I was fourteen years old in 1968 and was just in class just for us boys like shop Classes, and Phy-ed class and health class for boys only. This fact is true that I was forced to attend the very first co-ed Phy-ed and health class, and note I did not like to even be in this class at all, for I did not want to even learn about female health and growth and development.

Now the other classes that I did not even want to be in was the drama class, a girl's home education class, I was even forced to be in other things that are none academic things that the feminists and liberals wanted like the democrats and any one that had the same idea. It was also the time when the removal or the separation of gender was over.

Let us now take about co-ed Phy-ed class and health class for a little bit. Now I was forced to play field hockey which is a sport for girls only, but see that the liberal, feminist movement was starting to grow with the help of the liberals and democrats, and the demand that boys and girls should and could play the very same sports, and should play the very same sports.

Field hockey is not a sport for boys to play or to take part in, for this is a sport just for female to play only. In this case I was the only boy that was forced to play field hockey, and I had to wear a traditional field hockey uniform. I hated playing field Hockey, for I wanted to play football and sports like that, for these are sport just for boys to plat only.

I did not like being the only boy in home economics class for again this was a class for girls only and I did not want to learn how to sew or to make my own clothing.

Okay the class that I did not like was drama class, for the real reason was is that I did not want to be on stage and act in front of others. It was here in drama class where my shyness showed up the most, but that would change after September 7th 1968.

Before September 7th, 1968 we were studying Shakespeare and how all the males in Shakespeare's day had to play all the parts in not just his plays, but males had to play the female roles in every play in Shakespeare day as well. This is a historical fact no woman was allowed to even act on stage. Now what does this have to do with me, and just how did this change me from being a very shy boy to the man that I am today.

I do not recall the exact date it happened but I can recall this just a few days before

September 7th, 1968. Okay time to reveal just what did happen to change me from being a very shy boy to the man I am today.

I can recall sitting in class during a discussion and our teacher did ask a question to me directly to where my response was something that a feminist or a liberal and democrat would not like, and yes it was not bad words I said but it was words such as. Please note these are not my exact words, for I cannot recall them to this date, but I think I said "It is great that men or boys can no longer play girls or female roles in a play these day or today, and girls should be the ones that has to wear a dress or skirts only while on stage, and dancing and acting is not for a boy to-do." I am sure you get my point here that I said something that got my drama teacher very angry at me and I had to spend time in the principal's office for what I said.

Now I was facing a real problem here I was facing being expelled from school for not saying any bad language, but for making a remark to the fact a girl should play a girl's role in a play and a guy should be playing a guy's role only. In truth I did not know it at the time that both my drama teacher and principal were both feminist and liberals, and it was the day before September 7th, 1968.

To refresh your memories this is the even that did happen on September 7th, 1968 that did change me to what I am like to day and why I am the way I am as well today.

The event was the 1968 was ladies protesting the Miss America Beauty pageant of 1968, whereby women had a bra burning event and were demonstrating against the idea of having beauty contest and claiming it was degrading women around the world, or something like that.

The reason why I can recall this date so well was I was going to be punished for my comments or remakes I made in drama class.

Okay in drama class my teacher want to have us preform the musical play by Rodgers and Hammerstein's "Oklahoma" the 1955 movie version starring Sherry Jones as Laurey Williams.

Okay back to the punishment that was given out to me, and yes this idea was also the idea that came from my drama teacher and principal too. this time my parents did protest about me being punished this way and why I was to be punished at all, but to no avail, for I had to do it and do it well. Even my drama class had to go along with my punishment as well.

I was forced to play the role "Laurey Williams" who is one of the leading roles in the musical play "Oklahoma". Now after being told that I would have to play this role the shyness that was in me was over, for I spoken up and said things like this is wrong and I did not want to be in the play in the first place. I would rather be scenery or just one that made things or something else. I was even told that if I don't do this role I would be expelled from school and the only way for me to return to school is to wear a dress to school. As you can see either way I had to wear a dress no matter what. So I did just that very thing I agreed to play the role of "Laurey Williams" in the musical play "Oklahoma" in 1968.

Singing was not hard for me for my voice did not change for I still had that soprano or a very high male that sounded like I was a girl in the first place and I was also very thin as a boy as well.

Acting however was very hard for me, for I never wanted to be an actor or to even act on a stage in front of audience. I hated this idea so much I was thinking of ways not to do this role or even be on stage, but to no avail, for a surprise announcement was given to the class by our teacher and principal.

The announcement was this that I had to learn and preform the role as if I was Laurey

Williams, and if anyone was even caught bulling, or not helping me learn this role they too would be punished, and the girls in the class must teach and help me become a female, even the girls that wanted to play the role of Laurey Williams had to help in every way shape or form. There was one other thing that did happen too. The whole class even and this includes me as well had to keep this a secret from others, for our teacher want to have a surprise performance and to see if I could be a very good Laurey Williams. Our grade does depend on how well we as a class would perform on stage.

Learning the line and song for the play was not hard for me to do at all, but the hardest thing was getting fitted for my costumes, first thing was to fit me for costumes was from the time period 1906 before Oklahoma was a state in the union. So I had to now look like a lady from the time period 1906, and I also had to look like a farm girl too. to solve this one problem was easy for the school to do, for the school ask if costume and makeup designers and artic form the local group that are performer would come and help out as volunteers. I also had to overcome being very shy as well.

The very first costume that I was fitted for was the bloomers and undergarments that I was to wear in the play. The one thing that was hardest undergarment for me to wear was a corset. Okay not so hard for the one problem that had to be overcome was this fact. I was a flat chested boy, so I had to learn how to wear the corset with false breast.

Making breast for a fourteen year old girl was not hard for the makeup artic, for all she had to do was to make rubber looking breast that would fit me very well. Now a bra was put on me with the false breast for me to get use to while we were rehearing our parts under the dress that was picked out for me to wear during all of our rehearsals before dress rehearsals or our final rehearsals. Yes I had to even sit in class wearing a dress.

13

A wig was made just for me to wear. The wig was blonde and could be styled to make me look like a girl, plus I also had to wear the wig with the dress, bra and breast that were formed just for me to wear.

Now time came for me to get fitted and try on the dresses that I was to wear in the musical play "Oklahoma" as "Laurey Williams", and I wanted to hide because now I was going to wear a dress on stage.

When it came time for the fittings I always had to wear all the undergarments that was made for me to wear in the play, plus I found out just how hard it was for a woman to even move wearing those type of undergarments. Wearing the bloomers was the easiest for me to move about and comfortable from the beginning, and yes I got very use to wearing the costumes too.

Okay the corset was very easy for me to wear even at first, and I was made comfortable wearing that as well.

The first dress was a farm girl's style dress whereby I had to wear a petticoat, apron, well it was a skirt, with a nice white blouse; I was wearing white tights, accuse the bloomers, corset, white female boots that where laced up like they did in 1906, with heals. The color of the dress was a light purple white checkered squared. The petticoats were white and the bloomers and corset was also white.

The ladies boots that I was to wear hade to be made for me to wear and yes I had to break them in order for me to walk and wear them like a lady should. In truth I had to learn how to wear high heels and learn to walk wearing high heels. This I will tell you learning to dance in high heels were easy and I will tell you later. Note this there is a scene in the play where I would be just wearing the bloomers, corset, tights, and boots, plus be singing to the other girls only.

The next dress I was fitted for was the dream scene dress where I had to do some ballet in it. The ballet shoes are the only other shoes I was to wear in the musical play.

In the dream scene I did not have to wear the petticoats, for it was much easier for me to move and dance the simple ballet movements I had to perform in the play.

Yes all the girls that where in the play was with me in all the fitting of our costumes that we were to wear in the play it was not just me, but seeing that I had no idea how to even wear female cloth even a dress of that time period of the 1960's, I even had no idea of how to even wear a dress from 1906. Yes the girls would giggle and smirk seeing me wearing a dress and being fitted in my costumes. You should of seen there smiles and here their remarks too.

Next were my party dress and the same dress that I had to wear when Curly had to purpose marriage to me. The wedding dress was next fitting after that.

After all the fittings I had to wear makeup for the very first time, and yes that was very interesting thing, for I never wore any makeup at all before well seeing that I was a boy and boys never wear makeup at all.

I was told that I had to sit in the makeup chair with one of the costumes that fit me the best and it was the very first one the farm girl dress.

Now this is where I learned just how a professional makeup artic does work, for I first had something called a base or foundation and they call it a makeup fitting. This took over an hour to find the right foundation for me to wear. Having makeup applied would include the wig I was to wear.

Sitting in the makeup chair is a very interesting experience too, besides the face makeup I also had nail polish apply just to see the right colors or color for me to wear in the play.

Okay after all of the fittings and makeup none of the costumes where ready, but the undergarments, for the undergarments fit right away, but it was now time for me to learn just how to act like a girl.

The preparation was the hardest for me to do and learn, for example I had to learn how to stand, walk sit like a lady. Then it was the ballet for me, and for some reason this came to me very naturally I don't know' why. I even had to learn how to sit walk well even dance like a lady wearing high heel boots that where laced up from 1906.

I made friends while doing this play, for one of the girl's that wanted to play the part Laurey Williams became one of my best friends and we stayed friend after the play was over. She helped me out the most on how to be a girl or one could say a lady. She understood the problem I had, so she took me on the side from time to time just to teach me.

Now it was getting closer to doing the play and everyone was now settling into doing their parts. There was a photo shoot well stills of us in all of our costumes and we had to pose with for example me and the boy that was to paly Curly We took stills of me in the wedding dress with the boy that played Curly holding my hands as if we were just married, and him and I kissing, hugging as if we were a marriage couple. I had to sit on his lap.

Okay I did one thing to help me learn just how to be Laurey William and the only real model I had was Sherry Jones when she played Laurey Williams, for I would imitate her in truth, plus add the thing ours had taught me, and add my own ideas.

Now the moment of truth was opening night, for not one person other that the kids in my drama class and a few of my teachers know that Laurey Williams would be played boy a very shy fourteen year old boy.

The fear of being on stage was real and it was a nightmare for me, for now is the moment of truth for me for was I going to pass as a girl on stage and the other thing was I going to pass being Laurey Williams, and the other thing is how would the audience going to like the play? Those were the question that was going to be answered when I first start to sing

Now hearing the boy that played Curly sing "Oh, What a beautiful Mornin" was my very first hint of being real nervous and I had the fear of not going on stage, but I was told by my girlfriend to relax. Then I stepped on stage going through the door on Laurey's house singing "Oh, What a beautiful Mornin" with Curly then I got over being nervous and shy at the same time. Let say after that I relaxed and got through scene one of the play. Yes in scene one Curly and Laurey would tease each other about going to the box social dance and barn raising. In my mind at that time I was loving doing this, but I never and did not dare tell anyone that I love being Laurey Williams at that time.

The next part that I would appear in scene one was with Ado Annie she is a very pickled lady where she was in love with Will and a peddler. It was the peddler where Laurey buys a drug that will give Laurey the dream of her and Curly, with Jud and it was in that scene where I had to do the ballet dance.

There is one thing I should add, and it is this. I decided add one thing to my way of teasing the boy that played Curly. I would add a wiggle or sway my hips a little bit to show him that I was a tease. This was something that my teacher noticed and said some like that was great.

The very hardest song and scene for me to play was when the girls would come in the house to freshen up and everyone would be in their bloomer and corsets or just removing the petticoats like they did back in 1906 in order to freshen up. Now in the play I had to sing to them and the audience this song and "Many of New Days". The reason why it was hard was the fact I was singing it just to the girls while I was wear my petticoat, bloomers, tights, corset the undershirt under my corset that I was wearing and my high heel boots oh yes I put on a nice pink garter on both tights too.

I am very sure you can see where this would be very hard for me, because I am a boy and this is a scene just for a girl to play, plus the fact I was only a fourteen year old boy that was very shy until I did this play. Please always keep that in mind as you read even more.

I am going to kind of skip ahead just a little bit here to the scene where Curly does purpose to Laurey a marriage proposal and she does accept his proposal to be his bride and wife. I even added one other thing here I gave the boy that was playing the part Curly a very good and sexy kiss whereby we did not rehearse. Yes we did rehearse with a type of kiss that did not look to sexy, but I added a kiss that would do just that in this scene. I did this just to be funny and to add a little bit of humor to the scene. I was just acting at this time by doing this for the fear being on stage was gone from the opening.

The wedding scene was next and yes I even added this to what I was to be doing I put my head on Carly's shoulder and batted my eyes as if I was in love with him. Swaying my hips while dancing and singing help me out.

Okay at the end of the play it was time to take a curtain call, and yes I got a big surprise When the members of the cast in the play was finally introduced I was last one, and you know what I did not even want to go out for the curtain call, for on my mind was I am a boy wearing a wedding dress.

Yes I could hear the audience clapping and cheering as the cast members was being introduced, but with my fear two girl with the help of the boy that played Curly almost dragged me back out in front of the audience so that I could take a bow, but as my teach said "Playing Laurey Williams is me" then as my last name was said I saw my very first standing ovation.

Okay I had tears in my eyes as I saw the standing ovation, for I saw that the audience loved the play. The standing ovation did last at least five minutes I think. Even my parents were part of the standing ovation.

The next time in class there was one other announcement that the play went over so good that we are going to do more than the one night we did the play for almost one year.

Okay my mother wants to keep some of the still pictures of me in the play, and I just don't know how she did it she kept all the costume I wore in the musical play "Oklahoma" this would include my high heel boots that I wore, and the bridal flowers that I had in the play.

Okay I did hate playing the role Laurey Williams in the play and being a girl, for I am the type that does not like to be an actor or do any acting, but I enjoy watching plays and live musicals maybe one day I will see a musical play on Broadway someday, and yes I has seen live performances from local theater groups. I have even seen live performances productions of Oklahoma" too.

I would still say that a girl or lady should play a female role in a play and not a male, for female role are just for the ladies to do only. In addition a woman should never play the role that is for a male too. Wearing dresses and skirt are for women and girls only.

I would like to say if anyone would like to know just which one of the costumes that I like out of the four is the bridal dress, for it was the most comfortable one for me to wear, and please note that it was also the easiest for me to move around like dancing. Okay at first it was kind of weird for me to throw a bridal bouquet for the very first time, and also note it is not normal for a boy to even throw bridal bouquet too.

Chapter Three

Co-Ed

Now it is very interesting that as a boy that grew up in the 1960's and seeing that 1968 was a turning point in my life whereby I had to play a female role in what would have been a one night thing to whereby it lasted one year. Yet there was even more that did happen to me in the 1960's especially 1968 and 1969 whereby I did pass as a girl.

Okay playing the part as Laurey Williams in the musical play "Oklahoma" was one of them, but there was even more that did happen to me whereby I was mistaken as a girl in 1968, and yes there was other times and yes there was even more that maybe we should talk about in this chapter.

Now having a feminist as a drama teach was bad enough, but having another feminist as my Phy-Ed and health teach was very interesting as well, plus the fact I was the only boy in a class with all girls.

I you happen to recall that I said I was forced to play field hockey and I wish I could of played football instead. The truth is that would be true, for a boy or to a boy playing with girl and playing a girl's sport that should be played by girls only is not a dream or is not and was not fun.

As we can see that seeing that this is just what the liberals and democrats, plus it comes from President Johnson wanted where by all education had to be equal including the sport that we play or games that we play. This is one of the things that laws like Cal. Const. amend.chap.85. § § 221.5 (a)(b)(c)(d)(e)(f) or laws like having same-sex marriage is all about.

Now this is the way equal education and equal rights was to be according to both

President Kennedy and President Johnson wanted for not just public schools, but all schools like private, home, charter, church schools, and so forth. Another wise everything had to be like the communist way of education.

According to what liberals' democrats like President Kennedy and President Johnson every boy was the same as a girl and the girls are the same as a boy, for there is no difference in gender. The start of no gender identification did start in the 1960's with both President Kennedy, and President Johnson. It is this very reason why I had to play Laurey Williams and was forced in co-ed Phy-ed and co-ed health class whereby I was force to play field hockey, and wear the very same uniform as the girls did when they played field hockey.

The one question that was no answer yet is because of the fact now would be the time to Answer this very question how did I change into the field hockey uniform and my costumes that I had to wear in the musical play "Oklahoma" when I played the part "Laurey Williams"

It was kind of simple but also kind of hard as well, for at first I was told that I had to use the girls locker room when I had to change my clothes for both by my teachers and my principal, but before one gets in a up roar and say something here is one thing I had my teachers help me out by asking them for help on how I was to change my clothes.

For Phy-ed I had to change my clothes in the teacher office and shower in the teacher office after class was over and it was my Phy-ed/ health teacher did put my Phy-ed clothes in my locker that was in the girls' locker room. So you can see it was my teachers that had to do those things for me.

Now it was my Phy-ed teacher that was also in charge of cheerleaders and those that wanted to be a cheerleader. To tell you this I was not interested in being a cheerleader or even want to do anything with a cheerleader, for a cheerleader is for girls' only and not for any boy to do.

Seeing that I was not too bad in gymnastics well boys gymnastics and not girls gymnastics is why my Phy-ed/ cheerleader/health teacher wanted me to try to be a cheerleader. It was very good that I did not do very well here, well in truth I messed up trying to be a cheerleader for the reason I just did not feel like wearing the cheerleader uniform. I faked being bad that is my secret how to get out of the things that was meant for a girl.

If one just looks back in time one would see that I would have had to wear a female cheerleader's skirt. Now I was wearing a dress already in the school play musical as Laurey Williams, and was having this on my mind is playing the role Laurey Williams enough?

It is very crazy idea to have a shy boy like me in co-ed Phy-ed/ health class as a boy that did not want to be the only boy in a girls' Phy-ed /health class and just call it co-ed because of the fact the liberals and democrats want to see more co-ed class whereby it does not matter what one's gender (sexual orientation) is.

In truth I became afraid to even talk to males because of being in a co-ed Phy-ed/health class and yes I had more female friends and it made it much easier you me to even communicate with females, but I can say I did miss out on talking about male thing.

I can say it was nice and yes I have and always had respect on the growth and development of the female body, and the problems a woman has when she changes from adolescent to an adult female. Here is one thing I did learn was a period and the development of the girl's sexual biological clock that is in her. I would stare out the window in health class because I felt like I was not learning anything at all. I always felt that I would have to think and feel like a girl all the time, and is that the right thing to do is to force a boy into learning about how to be a female, or force a boy to be a girl?

I would like to go back to where I mentioned the Cal. Const. amend.chap.85. § § 221.5 (a)(b)(c)(d)(e)(f) just take a good look at this law that the liberals came up with in the State of California.

This one law is designed to do just what I went through in the 1960's and 1970's in school. Yes I went to public school where one would expect this type of law to be enforced or put in place. The real meaning of this law is it does not matter just what type of school whether it is a private, church, home, charter type of schools for example if a boy feels like a girl he can do or take part in what is for a girl only. Now this would mean what I went through in the 1960's and 1970's is okay and there is not one thing that anyone could do or say against a boy taking part in girls Phy-ed/health class in any school setting. The question I would have to have is why was I picked to be a forefather to the idea of co-ed, and why did not have a choice to take part in either boys Phy-ed or co-ed Phy-ed/health classes.

§ (a) of Cal. Const. amend.chap.85. § § 221.5 (a)(b)(c)(d)(e)(f) does spell all of this out in the fact that all schools no matter what must comply and the parents have no say to how the child is to be taught, or educated in any school. The law is a law of force or mandate, and is a government control law whereby the government has the right to control the development of a child. That is why Cal. Const. amend.chap.85. § § 221.5 (a)(b)(c)(d)(e)(f) is a law that would be a communist type of law.

Okay I am very sure you get my point here why co-ed Phy-ed/ health classes was very bad thing and a way that could affect the way a person thinking and development, plus shows why a boy is born as a boy only and the way he is born. This is also why a boy cannot be a girl or should be treated as if he was a girl. This why the title of my book is called What it was like being a boy and others thinking I was a girl in the 1960's, and yes I could include to even say the 1970's as well. I am very sure you could see my frustration and problem growing up with liberals and the liberal way of thinking and why the liberal way of thinking is so very wrong.

Now before Cal. Const. amend.chap.85. § § 221.5 (a)(b)(c)(d)(e)(f) became law in California in 2014 I was even force to change into my Phy-ed clothes in my teacher office at first, but later on in the year my teacher forced me to change in the girl's locker room. So this is why I was more accepted as a girl at school, and now you can know and understand what I have been leading up to all this time.

Now I love track and field especially running the 440 year dash, but in the 1960's track and field became more or less a co-ed type of sport, for it was beginning no longer be a boy only track team and just a girls track team it was going to be a co-ed track team whereby the girls and boys could train together as one team only.

Because of the fact my coach was a woman and she was very good at teaching me how to sprint; I had to always train with the girls, and in some track and field meets I had to race with the girls. Now this may seem okay, but remember that fact that I had to change in the girls' locker room for Phy-ed class, well the same thing went for me in track and field. My track coach was the same teacher I had for Phy-ed health class that is why.

My Phy-ed/health teacher was one of the ladies that was assigned to me to teach me how to be Laurey Williams for the musical play Oklahoma. She was the one who was assigned to teach me how to walk, and dance like a lady should. She even taught me how to curtsy with my dress on, and how to squat down instead of bending over like a boy would. So she did know about the punishment that would happen to me if I did not play the role Laurey William right and does a very good job play the role of Laurey Williams. There was even times when she would just call me Laurey only or miss Williams or just plain Laurey Williams instead on my real name. Okay I got very use to being called a Laurey by name or just by hearing the name Laurey, and I got used to it as well. When I heard my real name I did not know how to react from time to time because of the fact I was called Laurey more than my real name.

One day she did call me Laurey while in health class and yes I did answer her, and some of the girls just laugh at me because their just did not understand that I was to play the role Laurey Williams in the musical play Oklahoma just to keep from being expelled. She just forgot I think or I hope.

Daydreaming came very normal to me because I just wanted to get out of being in a co-ed Phy-ed/health class, and was the type of daydreams where I would be in a normal boys Phy-ed/health class instead of the girls Phy-ed/health class that was my dream. No I had no other type of daydreams but that type.

I can recall trying to get out of co-ed Phy-ed class by making up an excuse that I forgot my Phy-ed clothes. This was the wrong thing, for I now was force to wear girls' Phy-ed cloths that she had extras, for when I girl left clothing that was lost and never reclaimed she would keep them just in case, and now I had to wear the Phy-ed class that a girl would wear in the 1960's. the very ugly jumper style if you know just what I mean. This would include me wearing a bra, panties, girl's gym socks and shoes. Okay it was a training bra, but I was force to wear it. My lesson was never do that ever again. Now because of the experience I happen to feel sorry for you girl that have to wear those type of gym cloths for Phy-ed or any other thing too.

I did get punished as well and this punishment is part of my memory that I wish I could forget, for I forgot to tell you from time to time there was a gym clothing check to see and make sure that everyone was wearing the very same thing including required undergarments.

I got away with it until the very first uniform check was made, for my undergarments was the very same as a boy, and not the same as a girl would wear. The thing is all girls had to wear a bra, and panties with girl socks and shoes. I had no bra and panties on as undergarments. So I had to clean the shower in the girls' locker room.

Now in truth I never wore any bra or panties as my undergarments in my gym clothes, but I would always try to plain and figure out when an inspection would happen so that I would not have to clean the shower in the girls' locker room.

I was told by my teacher that she liked having me in her Phy-ed/health class, for this very reason why.

She said I was a very good student, and I would listen very well and do as I was told, and never complained about doing anything, and she felt or wish the other girls' was like me quite and one that wanted to learn. She even felt that I would fit in as a girl or with other girls, plus she even heard the girls like me in class. She could see to treat me like a girl was the way to go, and she hoped that I did enjoy the class too.

Chapter Four

A Weird Thing Began To Happen

Okay a very weird thing began to happen, for even while I was to play Laurey Williams in the musical play "Oklahoma" and even prior before and it happened more in the play Oklahoma I had some very strange feelings, for I was starting to thing that I was a girl.

Okay being dressed as a girl and allowed to pass as a girl is a bit strange for a boy in the 1960's and 1970's, yet if one does thing like one would today this is not even a bit strange at all. In today's society and way of liberal thinking if a boy wants to wear a dress or is forced to even look like a girl then it is okay, but keep in mind that very conservative would not even agree with the idea of seeing or having a boy even wear girl clothing at all.

The very weird thing did happen for my mother did keep all the costumes that I wore in The musical play Oklahoma is that she wanted to keep all the costumes and have copies of the picture that were taken of my being Laurey Williams. Okay I was still fourteen and I would have a desire to wear a dress or dress like a girl. This is a secret that I would keep until now that you can read it for your selves. It was a very great feeling trying on my costumes when I was a lone and yes I would sneak to the place where the costumes were kelp and put them on to have the feeling of just how I felt. As long as I could get in the dresses and wear everything else and the fact that they were my size, I would wear them just to feel like a girl like other thought I was, but I had a feeling of being beautiful.

While acting on stage I began to feel like a girl from the very first time on opening night of the play. My first kiss with the boy that played Curly made me feel like a girl instead of a boy. When I sang my song "A many of new day" to the girls on stage gave me the weird feeling of being a girl. The one fact was even when I was alone and practicing my lines and song I would pretend to be a girl each and every time. I would always have on my mind just how would Laurey feel or do the things I had to do while I was being her on stage.

Feeling trapped was just how I really felt, for I had the problem of being me, and now the problem of being a girl by the name of Laurey Williams too.

Yes it is true I would have to pass as a girl in the play on stage, and to try and convince the audience that I was a girl playing a female role in a play, but I felt like I was now trying to even convince myself that I was a girl too. this just how weird these feels were and how real these feeling were.

Everyone should know that these feeling in the 1960's and 1970's are not normal and was even forbidden to have as a boy. I know those how believe in these things are very normal like those liberals, feminist that like Cal. Const. amend.chap.85. § § 221.5 (a)(b)(c)(d)(e)(f) or is known as the California bathroom law.

Let me put one thing that is very clear to me and should be very clear to others that are not a liberal or a democrat the truth here is that all conservatives will know just how must things like a boy wearing a dress is wrong, and by reading the Cal. Const. amend.chap.85. § § 221.5 (a)(b)(c)(d)(e)(f) or as known as the California bath room law in the area that laws like these are very discriminatory to the boy or girl that does not choose to even agree with the idea of a boy wearing a dress or dressing up to look like a girl, and the very same thing does go for a girl if she feels like dressing or wanted to be a boy.

U.S.Const.amend.I "Congress shall make no law respecting an establishment of religion, or prohibiting the free exercise thereof; or abridging the freedom of speech, or of the press; or the right of the people peaceably to assemble, and to petition the government for a redress of grievances." Okay the people that say it is okay for a boy to dress like a girl is okay, for that does follow the guidelines of freedom of speech, and religion too for all forms of homosexuality, fumiest, liberals is a true form of religion, even being an atheist, or agnostic, even the ones that claim the United States of America so be free of religion like the "Freedom from Religion foundation" is a religion; for a hate group as such is included here as well, and here is why. Every human being no matter who they are has some type of believe in order to be alive, and has some form of believe that they do follow. To say you have no religion is a phony statement, and has no bases of fact[s].

Okay the whole meaning is yes it is an individual right[s] for a boy if he feelings like wearing girls' clothing such as a dress or skirt it should he right to do so according to the U.S.Const.amend.I, but if one does notice that it is wrong to force, mandate, or to even control or in my case I was forced to be in a play whereby I was forced to wear a dress and play a female role. It was against my very own will not to wear a dress and be the leading role in the musical play Oklahoma as Laurey Williams.

Now because of being forced to play the role as Laurey Williams or to be forced into co-ed in any way shape or form was a direct violation of my U.S.Const.amend.I rights and other United States Constitutional Amendments, plus other laws.

Seeing that everyone that would agree with the liberals, democrats, fumiest, homosexuals, boys that want to be a girl, or a girl that wants to be a boy is pure one hundred percent communism in it purist form and shape, for this is not freedom or even liberty.

Now one of the questions that could be asked is why all liberals and democrats do hate the idea of not having freedom and liberty and they love to call cross-dressing or just seeing a boy wear a dress or skirt as being freedom and liberty when in my case I was forced into wearing a dress.

29

Now just what does all of what was just said and these things have to do with a weird thing began to happen?

The weird thing that began to happen was I overcame being very shy to being very bold and now going against the liberals, feminists, democrats' way of thinking and rebelling against the ideas of the feminists, liberals, democrats of dealing with their very dumb and idiotic ideas for being gender neutral, or every human being having the same gender.

You see what happened to me was a violation of not just my U.S.Const.amend.I right, but my "Unalienable Right" that we can find U.S. Declaration of Independence, Paragraph 2 (1776) ""We hold these truths to be self-evident, that all men are created equal, that they are endowed by their Creator with certain unalienable Rights, that among these are Life, Liberty and the pursuit of Happiness.--That to secure these rights, Governments are instituted among Men, deriving their just powers from the consent of the governed, --That whenever any Form of Government becomes destructive of these ends, it is the Right of the People to alter or to abolish it, and to institute new Government, laying its foundation on such principles and organizing its powers in such form, as to them shall seem most likely to effect their Safety and Happiness."

Unalienable Rights are they rights that have been endowed by the Creator in which I have faith in. Now see that God is my Creator in whom I believe in; therefore it is the right for me to live life as a male and not to be forced to cross-dress or to pass as a female, or even have a mandate, or have another group or organization do like they did to me in the 1960's and 1970's.

It is not my idea to even pass or look like a girl in any shape way or form, even to act in a play or a musical.

Now you the reader can understand and see the point that by forcing me to do or think like a liberal, democrat, or a feminist, and by seeing that force is a communist idea and has never been change from my mind, and I will never ever change my mind over this one issue. The same would go for the California law Cal. Const. amend.chap.85. § § 221.5 (a)(b)(c)(d)(e)(f) (California Bathroom Law) which is a communist law.

It was a very stupid move on the feminists, liberals, and democrats doing this to me in very first place or any other boy that they tried things like this from that point onto the end of the earth.

Chapter Five

Let Us Review A Law The Was Made By The Communist Governor of California

Cal. Const. amend.chap.85. § § 221.5 (a)(b)(c)(d)(e)(f) or known as the "California Bathroom Law" is a law in which the State of California came enforce under U.S.Const.amend.X "The powers not delegated to the United States by the Constitution, nor prohibited by it to the states, are reserved to the states respectively, or to the people." This would be correct way to interoperate the Tenth Amendment that the States and People have the right to make and enforce a communistic law and a law that is not for the majority of the people.

As I understand this law the blind liberals, feminists, democrats just happen to say this law is based on equal rights. Okay that sounds good and a nice to have and see, but yet these groups of people hate to look at one thing that equal rights would have to say.

As a boy at the age of fourteen in 1968, and force to play the role in a musical play "Laurey Williams" in the Rodgers and Hammerstein's version "Oklahoma" as a school play.

After looking at one thing that freedom and liberty is all about we can truthfully say that the Cal. Const. amend.chap.85. § § 221.5 (a)(b)(c)(d)(e)(f) or known as the "California Bathroom Law" I would I should not of played the role of "Laurey Williams" in the school play.

Where in the Cal. Const. amend.chap.85. § § 221.5 (a)(b)(c)(d)(e)(f) or known as the "California Bathroom Law" is a hint of freedom or liberty for a boy to be a boy and to wear boy's clothing.

What this law does state is that if a boy wants to wear a dress or a skirt, or even play in a school play he can even if his parents do not wish or want him to do so. So now where is the freedom and "Unalienable Rights" of the parents, for the parents do have the "Unalienable Right" to have or force their son not to wear a dress or skirt.

Cal. Const. amend.chap.85. § § 221.5 (a)(b)(c)(d)(e)(f) or known as the "California Bathroom Law" is an immoral law, or it does promotes immorality and a very shameful life style of living. Note that all liberals, democrats, and communists just happen to love everything that is immoral, and immorality style of living; those the State of California is promoting that it is okay to ;live and be immoral plus it is okay to live in immorality too.

Now ever since the 1960's I saw thing like Cal. Const. amend.chap.85. § § 221.5 (a)(b)(c)(d)(e)(f) or known as the "California Bathroom Law" and other liberal, democrat as immoral and a communist as immorality; for it is unethical to live the way Cal. Const. amend.chap.85. § § 221.5(a)(b)(c)(d)(e)(f) or known as the "California Bathroom Law"

Okay this law was signed into law 2014 by California's Governor Brown who is a democrat and a liberal that is as so a left wing liberal who love to see every human being controlled by the government as if a human being is a slave.

Now it is time for repeating. Cal. Const. amend.chap.85. § § 221.5(a)(b)(c)(d)(e)(f) or known as the "California Bathroom Law" is legal and the State of California would have the right to enforce under U.S.Const.amend.X because of the words that is found in U.S.Const.amend.X, but the enforcement would have to come for the Executive Branch of California who is the Governor of the State of California.

Okay if the things would happen to me in the 1960's and 1970's such as in the musical play Oklahoma would I boy now classified as a girl v. a boy, or would I be forced live as a girl and stay cross-dress for the rest of my life?

It is was true then I would no longer have to do things and think like a boy; for it would be at the point in which my parents and I did agree to wear a dress and play the role Laurey Williams so that I would not be expelled from school; therefore I would no longer have any more

"Unalienable Rights" and I would no longer have any U.S.Const.amend.I rights according to Cal. Const. amend.chap.85. § § 221.5(a)(b)(c)(d)(e)(f) or known as the "California Bathroom Law" .

This would be truth that according to Cal.Const. amend.chap.85. § § 221.5(a)(b)(c)(d)(e)(f)or known as the "California Bathroom Law" all heterosexuals have no more Unalienable Rights at or any U.S.Const.amend.I rights because of the California bathroom law, because men like me would have to keep silence, and it would be a hate crime just to speak out against such immoral ideas and immorality like this at all.

Okay according to the rogue liberal Supreme Court judges the California bathroom law is the law and it is all in the name of equality and anti-discrimination, plus this would also mean those males are no longer to be classified as a male. This is also known a social justice, and social justice is a term that liberals, democrats are taking from the communist, for social justice is another type of demand, mandate, or way of control of the way we human beings are to live life. Where is the freedom and liberty to be free with the liberals and democrats with the help of the rogue liberal Supreme Court Judges makeup laws and removing our Unalienable Rights and our U.S.Const.amend.I rights?

There is no justice if the liberals, democrats, and rogue liberal Supreme Court judges are on the bench, and also in power in all three branches of governments; therefore just what good is it and any law[s] that promote immorality, unethical, and is a form of bulling by those that claim otherwise?

The one question that was not answered is this one about me in the 1960's and 1970's Why? Why me and why was I bullied by my liberal feminist principal, and teachers to be not a boy but to be a girl?

Okay the liberal feminist principal is dead and she cannot even answer those types of questions and I dare don't ask my liberal feminist drama teacher these type of questions and yes I just don't care to even ask the rest of the teachers that maybe still alive these types of question. So we would have to guess to just how they would answer these types of questions.

To answer one of the questions that was asked or inquired here in this chapter is to review and look at U.S.Const.art.III or the section in the United States Constitution that is the law[s] that are and just how the United States Supreme Court is to be controlled, and the rogue liberal judges are to obey.

U.S.Const.art.III, "§I The judicial power of the United States, shall be vested in one Supreme Court, and in such inferior courts as the Congress may from time to time ordain and establish. The judges, both of the supreme and inferior courts, shall hold their offices during good behaviour, and shall, at stated times, receive for their services, a compensation, which shall not be diminished during their continuance in office. §II The judicial power shall extend to all cases, in law and equity, arising under this Constitution, the laws of the United States, and treaties made, or which shall be made, under their authority;--to all cases affecting ambassadors, other public ministers and consuls;--to all cases of admiralty and maritime jurisdiction;--to controversies to which the United States shall be a party;--to controversies between two or more states;--between a state and citizens of another state;--between citizens of different states;-- between citizens of the same state claiming lands under grants of different states, and between a state, or the citizens thereof, and foreign states, citizens or subjects.
In all cases affecting ambassadors, other public ministers and consuls, and those in which a state shall be party, the Supreme Court shall have original jurisdiction. In all the other cases before mentioned, the Supreme Court shall have appellate jurisdiction, both as to law and fact, with such exceptions, and under such regulations as the Congress shall make.

The trial of all crimes, except in cases of impeachment, shall be by jury; and such trial shall be held in the state where the said crimes shall have been committed; but when not committed within any state, the trial shall be at such place or places as the Congress may by law have directed. §III Treason against the United States, shall consist only in levying war against them, or in adhering to their enemies, giving them aid and comfort. No person shall be convicted of treason unless on the testimony of two witnesses to the same overt act, or on confession in open court.

The Congress shall have power to declare the punishment of treason, but no attainder of treason shall work corruption of blood, or forfeiture except during the life of the person attainted."

The truth is all any Supreme Court judge can do is just interoperate the law[s], and the Supreme Court cannot make any law[s]. So where does a judge have the idea that they can make a law[s] by making it on the bench. No place or nowhere, for it is a direct violation of the law[s] for any judge to do so. That does answer the one question where is the problem the liberals, democrats have by say that the United States Constitution is a living document, whereby the United States Constitution is not a living document. Rogue judges should know and understand this.

By me saying all of this does prove that not just my U.S.Const.amend.I rights where Directly and delivery violated by the liberals, and feminist in the 1960's and 1970's, but even as we speak and write today as well.

Now under U.S.Const.art.II §4 we can have those judges, liberals democrats that are In power right now removed as it is written, for this is the part of the law that says so "§4The President, Vice President and all civil officers of the United States, shall be removed from office on impeachment for, and conviction of, treason, bribery, or other high crimes and

36

misdemeanors." Yes you that are liberals, democrats, and others that happen to agree with these groups need to lean and learn it well that the Constitution of the United States of America is the law[s] and you must obey it at all cost. The United States Constitution is not a living document.

Personal I do not care if a boy wear a dress or not, or if a girl wants to feel like she was born a boy and wants to live life in an immoral way with their idea of being a person of immorality. Just quit forcing the immorality and immoral way of life you choose to me and the rest of the world.

Chapter Six

God Does Not Goof

In truth this chapter is for all you that are liberal, and a democrat, and with a secular way of thinking, and to those who just don't believe in God, or any religion of any type.

God does not goof and will never make any mistakes at all like all you liberals, democrats, atheist, agnostics, freedom from religion, homosexual, same-sex marriage, cross-dressers, LBGTs, gays, and others that believe it is okay for a boy to wear a dress or skirt, or have a boy like me play a female in a school play, and so forth. Where do you get the idea from that God goofed when a boy in his mother's womb should have been a girl instead of being born a boy?

God is the only being that is pure and Holly and everything about God is pure righteousness making Him justifiably in his right to create you as a boy or a girl in your own mother's womb.

The fact is if you are a boy then you were born into this world for a reason, and you cannot and must not even change the way you are born, for if you do then you alone have violated to one and only truth that there is, for the day you change or want to change makes you a liberal and a liberal is an immoral human being.

Note those feminist liberal teachers and principals that wanted to force me to change and wear female clothing or to even act like a girl is and are all immorality unethically wrong. To force a boy like me to do things the way of a liberal or a democrat such as making me cross-dress even on stage whereby I wanted to reject and not do is a violation of my rights to be a male, and yes God will deal with you in His own way and in His own time period.

Even the liberal rogue Supreme Court judges that want to make their own law[s] as they feel fit to do in the name "equality" God will deal with you as well, for on that day you will cry out "Lord, Lord have mercy on me please. You rogue liberal judges will find out that God does not goof like you would believe, and keep in mind that God is pure and Holly making Him righteous, and the only one that can judge just how we human beings are to be. Only a liberal will rebel against God, and just ask Satan just what a liberal is, for he is one too.

There are those such as liberal Christians happen to say that God can goof and it is okay for a boy to wear a dress or a skirt; well the liberal Christian is no more a feel good type of occult group just making claim without any proof, facts, or any truth to even backup their claim, plus a liberal christian is just saying what it is saying just to please the none Christian organizations like those who believe in "freedom from religion foundation" for an example. Note that a liberal Christian does not have any faith in God nor do they even believe in God. This very same group does believe in same-sex marriage as well without any legal proof, facts, or even any truth to even backup their claims.

Let me put one thing very clear in just what I am saying here and if you that are parents of a boy or girl that wants to be the other gender in which they were born with or to and are allowing this to happen and say it is very normal then you parents are saying it is okay to have your very own children to like a very immoral life style, and you are also saying that immorality is okay as well. Those parents that would happen to disagree with me in the above statement you would be a liar and a thief for you are stealing for God has given to you and you are commending truth and a fact of life, plus you are a murder as well, for example if you happen to allow you son to wear dresses or a skirt and say it is okay then you have murdered your son and his way of life to live as a male. The same would go if you allow your daughter to do the very same thing if she wants to be a boy. This statement would be truth as well that you that are parents of said children are also a violator of moral humanity. Parents you have a responsibility, and should be also had accountable of the welfare of your children, and the harm that they may or have caused by thinking they are the other gender that they were born with.

One can find the very statement that I made in the Bible throughout the Bible and God does not like the idea of a boy or girl even thinking that he goofed when it comes to the gender of a child in its mother's womb. In the book of Genesis God does destroy the earth by bring out a worldwide flood because of homosexuality and other sexual immorality plus other immoral things that happens to come from homosexuality. God does destroy two cities because of homosexuality. God does warn about boys' wearing female clothing in the book of Deuteronomy the twenty-eighth chapter, and gives the very same warning to ladies that want to wear male clothing. In the New Testament God does warn about the very same thing and God does give parents instructions on how to raise up their children like for example in the Book of Ephesians chapter four and five.

Let's put it this way God gives us human beings these warnings not out of hate like the none believing world want to believe, but out of something that us human beings will never fully understand, and what us human beings will never fully understand is His love. This is called Holly love. This is the love that will surpass all human understanding, and is not fond in our hearts and minds. Here is why.

All human being are born with hate, and doing all things in an evil way, for this is way everything that is against God is called being a liberal, and a liberal is a rebellious human being the best example is a democrat, for they are the most rebellious human being that the world will ever know.

Let me put what I said in another way that most or all of you should understand. Satan is the most rebellious being in the whole wide universe, and many of you out there love to follow Satan without even thing about it, for this is how Satan gets you that are liberal to go against God with this very question he would ask you every single time. "Did God real say?" note this si the very question you that are liberal and don't believe in God happen to say when you ask the very question "Did God Goof when he created a boy in his mother's womb and the very same question goes for a girl in their mother's womb as well.

Liberals, democrats, atheist, agnostics, freedom from religion, homosexual, same-sex marriage, cross-dressers, LBGTs, gays, and others that believe it is okay for a boy to wear a dress or skirt, or have a boy like me play a female in a school play, and so forth. You are just as guilty as the parents that allow the children to think they should have been born the opposite gender instead of the gender that the child was born with. As human beings all of us are to be held accountable and responsible for the growth and development of a childs mind, and physical body, for the child is also under the care of every human being as well. This would go for those that never had a child or any children to rise, and those that do not want to have a child of their own.

The truth is God will never goof or make any mistakes for He is pure and Holly with a loving heart.

Parents bring your children or child up in a very respectful and loving way and this fact is truth, for there are four different types of love and the ways are found in the Greek.

Agápe (ἀγάπη agápē[1]) means "love: esp. brotherly love, charity; the love that comes from God. Éros (ἔρως érōs) means "love, mostly of the sexual passion. This is the type of love that all or most in todays would think love means especially here in the United States of America or those that speak English, for there is no interpretation of the word love in English.

41

Philia (φιλία *philía*) means "affectionate regard, friendship," usually "between equals. All those that are liberal in mind see the words "between Equals" to say it is okay to be an liberals, democrats, atheist, agnostics, freedom from religion, homosexual, same-sex marriage, cross-dressers, LBGTs, gays, and others that believe it is okay for a boy to wear a dress or skirt, or have a boy like me play a female in a school play, and so forth. They love to confuse the words between equals as to say it is okay to be immoral and to have immorality like they would like to do. Now for the last Greek word in our definition of the word love Storge (στοργή *storgē*) means "love, affection" and "especially of parents and children.

It is Éros (ἔρως *érōs*) that all liberals, democrats, atheist, agnostics, freedom from religion, homosexual, same-sex marriage, cross-dressers, LBGTs, gays, and others that believe it is okay for a boy to wear a dress or skirt, or have a boy like me play a female in a school play, and so forth, and this would include those that follow the religion of psychology, for eros is the only word they will only understand just like a true liberal would, and it is eros that brings about the hate all liberals would have. Sexuality is not just away to show love.

Chapter Seven

Conclusion

If you are wandering why in the 1960's and 1970's just what is was like being a boy and having others think I was a girl, or to have those in charge of me like a teacher[s] and my principal think it was okay to have me wear girl's clothing or to even act like a girl and the act in meaning here is not in a school play I mean here is being famine in nature.

After reviewing and thinking a lot about when I played Laurey Williams in the musical play Oklahoma I must confess I did enjoy it, and yet on the other hand I wish I have never played that role. Now I did learn something's when I did play the role Laurey Williams, for one thing I did learn was to do my best to try any imitate how to be a proper female when forced to be dress as a girl. I also did this all the time and one my see this toady as not a problem. I asked when I had to go to the bath room when I was dressed as Laurey Williams if it was okay and if someone would come and help me out or mainly to keep watch so that I would not get into trouble, for on my mind was this all the time. I did not like to even enter the girls' bath room or locker room even if I was dressed or about to change into my costumes as Laurey Williams. I was afraid of maybe seeing something that I should not have seen, and I was very shy still and yes getting over being shy. Even at the age of fourteen I always wanted to be a gentleman and do things the right way. This fact is true; I was able to use the girls' bath room when I was dressed as Laurey Williams and yes I got the help I need for the just incases. My Drama teacher and some of the other girls' would keep watch for me and keep other girls out until I was done doing whatever I was doing. When it came time for me to either change into or to change back into my own clothing again I had help and there was always some female to help keep watch. All of what I just said should tell you the reader the type of safety precautions that where taken for me.

As you can tell I did not say or tell you the reader everything or any real details for this reason. I never tell everything and I think you can get the main idea of just what it was like for me in 1960's and 1970's how I felt when people thought that I was a girl.

The one reason why I felt that co-ed Phy-ed/ health class was ridiculously bad, for again being a very shy boy and just getting over being so shy should tell you the reader that I was more at home if I would have been allowed to be in just boys Phy-ed/health class where I would be able to learn more about me and the male body development even more. How would you feel if you were told that you had to wear the very same uniform for gym class as the rest of the girls?

Field hockey as everyone should know is a sport that is to be played by females only and not by a male, or have the male wear a field hockey uniform only.

I know I did not talk or write about what it was like for me in the home economics class that was just for girls only. The reason why I never said anything was because I was forced to make a dress or a skirt, and I do not like to even sew any clothing. Making the dress that I never did wear well. You would understand my feelings over that. I would purposely ask for help when I made my dress, and yes my mother did keep this dress like she kelp all my costume that I had to wear in Oklahoma as well as the pictures too and any films that were made.

Cal. Const. amend.chap.85. § § 221.5 (a)(b)(c)(d)(e)(f) or known as the "California Bathroom Law" yes is a liberal law that does have an effect in California's education, but also has an effect in the area that adopt it as a law, and yes I happen to disagree with this law because it is a force, mandate, control law just like an law that comes from the communist style of government. You see liberals and the democrats love this way and type of government (Communist Control). Now if this law was in place in the 1960's and 1970's even though I did not cross-dress in my private life as a child or now an adult, and I will never even cross-dress nor will I even allow anyone to be around me in my circle, or an employee of mine to cross-dress for example a male will not be allowed to wear a dress if that male was an employee of mine. The male would be fired right on the spot. Now see that I was forced to cross-dress even when I was not in the school play Oklahoma as Laurey Williams. Take a good look at when I was in Phy-ed wear a field hockey uniform, and being asked to be a cheerleader and to wear the very same uniform as a cheerleader. Now that is force and you should know right now just what force means. And how the word force means in government.

Here is a fact as you have read my book so far. Have you noticed that I have never said the words hate or even said one thing that would be considered as hate?

Here is a fact there is not one person that I would even hate if they just like to cross-dress in front of me. Now speaking out against some idea or something like example a boy wearing a dress in public well in a public school is a good thing and should be a warning to the government and why it is wrong. Now if you notices that I will use an cite to back up my proof that a boy for example wearing a dress or skirt is just plain wrong. If you noticed that I said it is up to the individual if they even want to cross-dress or think they were born in the wrong body at the time of their conception. Yes it is a liberal worldview to say it is okay for a boy to cross-dress in public such as a public school.

Now the liberal worldview would say I hate those that want to cross-dress in public such as a public school for example, but this is the way a liberal worldview person does think and will always think like a blind person does. In truth they have never even heard me say anything in public therefore they are like the deaf. There is no love for others in a liberal worldview, for a liberal worldview is no more than pure one hundred percent hate, and that hate is for themselves all the time. A liberal worldview says "it is all in the name of equality" but in truth is it not in the name of "equality" at all. For it is in the name of control and a way to give up a thing called entitlements only so that the liberal can control you the reader of this book.

Liberals thrive on entitlements so that they can tax and tax the poor and middle class so that they can control everyone in the way they do things and the way we think too. Now you can see and read it for yourself that cross-dressing is not even the desire of the liberal worldview it is the fact that now they have a way to control like the communist can.

I did give you the reader the laws in my bibliography just so that you the reader of this book has am idea of just where I got my cites to back up just what I am saying in this book and what laws does backup with I am saying and just where I am coming from to help guide you.

Now God does not goof or makes any mistakes, for He is pure and Holly.

Bibliography

Cal. Const. amend.chap.85. § § 221.5 (a)(b)(c)(d)(e)(f)

U.S. Declaration of Independence, Paragraph 2 (1776)

U.S.Const.art.II §4

U.S.Const.art.III

U.S.Const.amend.I

U.S.Const.amend.X

www.ingramcontent.com/pod-product-compliance
Lightning Source LLC
Chambersburg PA
CBHW041518280526
45792CB00004B/1298